Chapter 1

Welcome to the World of eBay

eBay is more than just an online marketplace; it's a dynamic ecosystem that has revolutionized commerce on a global scale. With millions of active users and a vast array of products, eBay offers unparalleled opportunities for sellers to thrive and succeed. In this chapter, we'll dive into the essence of eBay, exploring its origins, its evolution, and why it has become the go-to platform for entrepreneurial spirits worldwide.

Introduction to eBay: A Global Marketplace Revolutionizing Commerce

eBay started as a humble experiment in online trading, founded by Pierre Omidyar in 1995. From its modest beginnings as AuctionWeb, where Omidyar originally wanted to create an online marketplace for the sale of goods between individuals, eBay has grown into a behemoth of e-commerce, connecting buyers and sellers across continents.

The platform's unique auction-style listings initially set it apart, allowing individuals to bid on items and negotiate prices in real-time. Over the years, eBay expanded its offerings to include fixed-price listings, stores, and even a global shipping program, catering to the diverse needs of sellers and buyers alike.

The Rise of eBay Sellers: From Hobbyists to Millionaires

What sets eBay apart is its democratizing effect on entrepreneurship. Unlike traditional brick-and-mortar businesses that require significant capital investment, eBay offers a low barrier to entry, allowing anyone with an internet connection and a product to sell to become an eBay seller.

Many successful eBay sellers started as hobbyists, selling items from their personal collections or crafting handmade goods in their spare time. With dedication, strategic thinking, and a deep understanding of the platform, these sellers transformed their side hustles into lucrative businesses, achieving millionaire status in the process.

Exciting Opportunities Await: Why eBay is the Platform for Entrepreneurial Success

eBay's vast reach and diverse user base make it an ideal playground for aspiring entrepreneurs. Whether you're a seasoned business owner looking to expand your online presence or a newcomer seeking your first taste of e-commerce success, eBay offers a level playing field where innovation and determination reign supreme.

In the pages that follow, we'll delve deeper into the strategies, tactics, and mindset needed to navigate the ever-changing landscape of eBay and emerge not just as successful sellers, but as millionaires in your own right. So, buckle up and get ready to embark on a journey that could transform your life and your bank account forever. Welcome to the world of eBay, where dreams are bought and sold every day.

Chapter 2

Setting Up Your eBay Seller Account

Welcome to the exciting world of eBay selling! In this chapter, we'll guide you through the essential steps of setting up your eBay seller account, laying the foundation for your journey towards becoming a successful eBay millionaire.

1. Understanding eBay's Seller Types:

Before you dive into setting up your seller account, it's crucial to understand the different types of seller accounts available on eBay:

- ➢ Personal Account: Ideal for casual sellers who plan to sell items occasionally.
- ➢ Business Account: Suited for individuals or entities intending to sell items regularly as a business.

Choosing the right type of account depends on your selling goals and volume. If you're serious about building a thriving eBay business, a Business Account provides access to additional tools and features tailored to meet your needs.

2. Creating Your eBay Seller Account:

Now, let's walk through the steps of creating your eBay seller account:

- Go to eBay's website: Navigate to eBay's homepage and click on the "Register" or "Sign Up" button.
- Enter your information: Provide your name, email address, and create a password for your account.
- Verify your identity: eBay may require you to verify your identity through email or phone verification to ensure security.
- Choose your seller type: Select whether you want to create a Personal or Business Account based on your selling intentions.
- Provide business information (if applicable): If you're creating a Business Account, you'll need to provide additional details such as your business name, address, and contact information.

3. Setting Up Payment Methods and Policies:

Once your eBay seller account is created, it's time to configure your payment methods and selling policies:

- Link your PayPal account: PayPal is eBay's preferred payment method, offering convenience and security for both buyers and sellers. Link your PayPal account to your eBay seller account to receive payments seamlessly.
- Set up shipping and return policies: Define your shipping options, including shipping carriers, handling time, and shipping rates. Additionally, establish clear

return policies to provide transparency and build trust with your customers.

4. Creating Your Seller Profile:

Your seller profile is your opportunity to showcase your credibility and professionalism to potential buyers. Here's how to optimize your seller profile:

- ➤ Upload a profile picture: Choose a professional-looking photo that represents your brand or business.
- ➤ Write a compelling bio: Craft a brief yet informative bio that highlights your expertise, experience, and commitment to customer satisfaction.
- ➤ Add contact information: Provide accurate contact details, including an email address and phone number, to facilitate communication with buyers.

5. Listing Your First Item:

With your eBay seller account set up, it's time to list your first item for sale:

- ➤ Click on "Sell" :Navigate to the "Sell" section of your eBay account dashboard.
- ➤ Enter item details: Describe your item accurately, including its title, description, condition, and photos.

- Set a price: Determine the price at which you want to sell your item, considering factors such as market demand, competition, and condition.
- Select shipping options: Choose your preferred shipping method and specify any additional shipping details, such as international shipping or expedited delivery.
- Review and publish: Double-check your listing details for accuracy and completeness before publishing your listing live on eBay.

Congratulations! You've successfully set up your eBay seller account and listed your first item for sale. As you continue your eBay selling journey, remember to stay engaged with your customers, maintain high-quality listings, and adapt to market trends to maximize your success and reach your millionaire goals.

Understanding eBay's Policies and Guidelines

Navigating eBay's policies and guidelines is crucial for every seller to ensure a smooth and successful selling experience. Here's a detailed overview to help you grasp the essentials:

1. Seller Standards and Performance Expectations:

eBay maintains strict seller standards to uphold trust and integrity within its marketplace. These standards encompass various aspects of your selling performance, including:

- Feedback Score: Your feedback score reflects your reputation as a seller, based on buyer feedback and ratings. Aim to maintain a high feedback score by delivering exceptional customer service and promptly resolving any issues.

- ➢ Defect Rate: eBay monitors your defect rate, which includes factors such as cases opened against you for item not as described, late shipments, and canceled orders. Keeping your defect rate low is essential for maintaining good standing as a seller.

- ➢ On-Time Shipping: Timely shipping is vital to meet buyer expectations and avoid penalties. Strive to ship orders promptly and provide accurate tracking information to buyers.

2. Listing Policies and Restrictions:

eBay has specific policies governing what items can and cannot be sold on its platform. Understanding these policies is crucial to avoid listing violations and potential account suspension. Key aspects include:

- ➢ Prohibited and Restricted Items: eBay prohibits the sale of certain items, such as counterfeit goods, weapons, drugs, and hazardous materials. Additionally, certain items may be restricted based on legal or safety concerns. Familiarize yourself with eBay's prohibited and restricted items list to ensure compliance.

> Listing Practices: eBay maintains guidelines for creating listings, including rules for item descriptions, photos, and pricing. Ensure your listings are accurate, detailed, and comply with eBay's policies to provide a positive shopping experience for buyers.

3. Selling Fees and Payment Policies:

As an eBay seller, it's essential to understand the fees associated with selling on the platform and eBay's payment policies. Key considerations include:

> Final Value Fees: eBay charges a final value fee based on the total selling price of your item, including shipping costs. Familiarize yourself with eBay's fee structure to accurately calculate your selling expenses and optimize your pricing strategy.

> Payment Processing: eBay primarily uses PayPal for processing payments, although alternative payment methods may be available in some regions. Ensure your PayPal account is linked to your eBay seller account to receive payments seamlessly. Additionally, be aware of PayPal's transaction fees and processing times.

4. Customer Service and Resolution Processes:

Providing excellent customer service is essential for maintaining buyer satisfaction and resolving any issues that may arise. eBay offers various tools and resources to help sellers address buyer concerns effectively, including:

> ➢ Resolution Center: eBay's Resolution Center allows buyers and sellers to communicate and resolve disputes regarding transactions, such as item not received or item not as described cases. Promptly respond to inquiries and work collaboratively with buyers to find mutually beneficial solutions.

> ➢ Returns and Refunds: eBay's return policy dictates the terms and conditions for accepting returns and issuing refunds to buyers. Establish clear return policies in your listings and adhere to eBay's guidelines for processing returns and refunds promptly.

By understanding and adhering to eBay's policies and guidelines, you can build a reputation as a trustworthy seller, mitigate risks, and create a positive selling experience for your customers. Take the time to familiarize yourself with eBay's rules and regulations, and always prioritize transparency, honesty, and professionalism in your interactions with buyers.

Choosing Your Niche: Finding Your Profitable Corner

Selecting the right niche is a critical step in building a successful eBay business. Your niche determines the types of products you'll sell, the target audience you'll cater to, and ultimately, your potential for profitability. Here's an in-depth guide to help you choose your niche wisely:

1. Assess Your Interests and Expertise:

Start by considering your personal interests, passions, and expertise. What are you knowledgeable about? What hobbies or activities do you enjoy? Your niche should align with your interests to keep you motivated and engaged in your business. Additionally, your existing knowledge and expertise can give you a competitive edge in your chosen niche.

2. Research Market Demand and Competition:

Conduct thorough market research to evaluate the demand and competition within different niches on eBay. Use eBay's advanced search features, including completed listings and sold items, to analyze the popularity and profitability of various product categories. Pay attention to factors such as:

- ➢ Search Volume: Look for niches with a high volume of searches and sales to indicate strong demand from buyers.

- ➢ Competition Level: Assess the level of competition within each niche, considering the number of sellers, listing quality, and pricing strategies. Aim for niches with manageable competition where you can differentiate yourself effectively.

- ➢ Trends and Seasonality: Identify trends and seasonal fluctuations in demand for different product categories.

While seasonal niches can be profitable during peak periods, consider whether your chosen niche has year-round appeal to sustain long-term growth.

3. Identify Profitable Product Opportunities

Once you've narrowed down your niche options, delve deeper into specific product opportunities within each niche. Look for products that meet the following criteria:

- ➢ Profit Margin: Evaluate the profit potential of each product based on factors such as sourcing cost, selling price, and associated fees. Aim for products with healthy profit margins that justify your time and effort.

- ➢ Sourcing Accessibility: Consider the ease of sourcing products within your chosen niche. Look for reliable suppliers or sources where you can access inventory consistently and cost-effectively.

- ➢ Unique Selling Proposition (USP): Identify opportunities to differentiate your products from competitors by offering unique features, superior quality, or exceptional value. Your USP should resonate with your target audience and give them a compelling reason to choose your listings over others.

4. Consider Target Audience Preferences:

Understand the preferences, needs, and pain points of your target audience within your chosen niche. Tailor your product selection and marketing strategies to address these preferences effectively. Consider factors such as:

> Demographics: Identify the demographics of your target audience, including age, gender, location, and income level. Customize your product offerings and messaging to resonate with your target demographic.

> Psychographics: Consider the psychographic characteristics of your audience, such as lifestyle, interests, and values. Appeal to their aspirations, desires, and pain points through your product selection and branding.

5. Test and Iterate:

Finally, don't be afraid to test different niches and product offerings to find what works best for your eBay business. Start with a small selection of products within your chosen niche and monitor their performance closely. Analyze sales data, customer feedback, and market trends to refine your niche selection and product assortment over time.

Choosing the right niche is a strategic decision that can significantly impact the success of your eBay business. By thoroughly researching market demand, assessing your interests and expertise, and understanding your target audience, you can identify a profitable corner of the market where you can thrive as an eBay seller. Remember to stay adaptable and open to experimentation as you refine your niche selection and build your business for long-term success.

Chapter 3: Building Your Brand on eBay

Crafting Your Unique Selling Proposition (USP)

In the competitive landscape of eBay, having a strong Unique Selling Proposition (USP) is essential for distinguishing your listings from competitors and attracting buyers. Your USP communicates the unique value and benefits of your products, compelling customers to choose your listings over others. Let's delve into the intricacies of crafting a compelling USP:

1. Understand Your Target Audience:

Before crafting your USP, it's crucial to understand the needs, preferences, and pain points of your target audience. Conduct market research to gain insights into your audience's demographics, psychographics, and purchasing behavior. Identify what motivates them to buy and how your products can fulfill their needs better than competitors.

2. Analyze Your Competitors:

Study your competitors' listings to identify gaps, weaknesses, and opportunities in the market. Evaluate their USPs, pricing strategies, product offerings, and customer feedback. Look for areas where you can differentiate yourself and offer unique value propositions that resonate with your target audience.

3. Identify Your Unique Value Proposition:

Your unique value proposition is the essence of your USP – it defines what sets your products apart and why customers should choose them. To identify your unique value proposition, consider the following:

- ➤ Product Features and Benefits: Highlight distinctive features, attributes, or benefits of your products that competitors don't offer or emphasize. Focus on aspects that address your audience's specific needs or preferences.

- ➤ Quality and Reliability: Emphasize the quality, craftsmanship, and reliability of your products. Assure customers of their durability, performance, and satisfaction, reinforcing trust and credibility in your brand.

- ➤ Exceptional Customer Service: Position your customer service as a key differentiator, offering personalized support, fast response times, and hassle-free resolutions to inquiries or issues. Demonstrate your commitment to customer satisfaction and building long-term relationships.

4. Communicate Your USP Effectively:

Once you've defined your unique value proposition, it's essential to communicate it effectively across your eBay listings and marketing channels. Here's how to convey your USP clearly:

- ➤ Compelling Product Descriptions: Craft persuasive product descriptions that highlight your USP and its benefits to customers. Use descriptive language, storytelling, and persuasive techniques to engage buyers and compel them to make a purchase.

- ➤ High-Quality Visuals: Enhance your listings with high-quality images and videos that showcase your products in the best light. Highlight key features, details, and use cases to reinforce your USP visually and capture buyers' attention.

- ➤ Branding and Messaging: Infuse your branding and messaging with your USP, conveying a consistent message across all touchpoints. Incorporate your unique value proposition into your brand story, taglines, and marketing materials to reinforce brand identity and differentiation.

5. Test and Refine:

Continuous testing and refinement are essential for optimizing your USP and its effectiveness in driving sales. Monitor the performance of your listings, analyze customer feedback, and experiment with different messaging and strategies to identify what resonates best with your audience.

Crafting a compelling USP takes time, research, and creativity, but the payoff is invaluable – increased visibility, customer loyalty, and sales growth on eBay. By understanding your audience, analyzing competitors, and effectively communicating your unique value proposition, you can differentiate your brand and position yourself for success in the competitive eBay marketplace.

Creating Compelling Product Listings

The success of your eBay business hinges on the effectiveness of your product listings. Compelling listings not only attract buyers but also compel them to make a purchase. In this section, we'll explore the key elements of crafting compelling product listings that captivate your audience and drive sales:

1. Write Engaging Titles:

The title is the first thing buyers see when browsing eBay, making it crucial for grabbing their attention. Here's how to create engaging titles:

- Be Descriptive: Clearly describe the item using relevant keywords that buyers are likely to search for.

- Highlight Key Features: Include important details such as brand, model, size, color, and condition in your title to provide buyers with essential information at a glance.

- Use Keywords Strategically: Incorporate relevant keywords that align with your target audience's search queries to improve visibility and search ranking.

2. Craft Compelling Product Descriptions:

A well-written product description provides buyers with detailed information about your item and helps them make an informed purchasing decision. Here are some tips for crafting compelling product descriptions:

- Be Descriptive: Provide a thorough description of the item, including its features, specifications, dimensions, and any relevant details that buyers need to know.

- Highlight Benefits: Focus on the benefits and value propositions of your product, explaining how it solves a problem or fulfills a need for the buyer.

- Use Persuasive Language: Use persuasive language to entice buyers and create a sense of urgency or excitement. Highlight unique selling points, special features, or limited-time offers to encourage immediate action.

3. Showcase High-Quality Images:

Visuals play a critical role in enticing buyers and showcasing your products effectively. Follow these guidelines for creating compelling product images:

- ➢ Use High-Quality Photos: Capture clear, well-lit photos that accurately represent your item's appearance and condition. Use a high-resolution camera or smartphone and ensure images are in focus and free of clutter.

- ➢ Show Multiple Angles: Include multiple photos from different angles to give buyers a comprehensive view of the item. Highlight key features, details, and any imperfections to set accurate expectations.

- ➢ Include Zoomable Images: Enable the zoom feature on your images to allow buyers to inspect the item closely and evaluate its quality.

4. Provide Detailed Product Specifications:

In addition to the description, include detailed product specifications to provide buyers with essential information. Consider including the following details:

- Dimensions and Size: Specify the item's dimensions, size, weight, and any relevant measurements to help buyers assess suitability and compatibility.

- Material and Construction: Describe the materials, construction, and manufacturing processes used in the item's production to convey quality and durability.

- Compatibility and Compatibility: If applicable, specify compatibility with other products or devices to ensure buyers make informed purchasing decisions.

5. Set Clear Pricing and Shipping Information:

Transparency is key when it comes to pricing and shipping information. Be upfront about costs and delivery expectations to avoid surprises for buyers. Here's how:

- Set Competitive Pricing: Research market prices and competitors' listings to set a competitive yet profitable price for your item.

- Specify Shipping Options: Clearly outline your shipping options, including carriers, delivery times, and any additional fees. Offer expedited shipping or free shipping options to attract buyers and improve conversion rates.

By implementing these strategies, you can create compelling product listings that capture buyers' attention, instill confidence, and ultimately drive sales for your eBay business. Remember to regularly monitor and optimize your listings based on buyer feedback, market trends, and performance metrics to maintain a competitive edge in the marketplace.

Utilizing High-Quality Images and Descriptions

In the competitive world of e-commerce, high-quality images and descriptions are your best tools for capturing the attention of potential buyers and convincing them to make a purchase. In this section, we'll explore how to effectively utilize high-quality images and descriptions to enhance your eBay listings and drive sales:

1. Capturing High-Quality Images:

a. Invest in Equipment: While you don't need professional photography equipment, investing in a good camera or smartphone with a high-resolution camera can significantly improve the quality of your images.

b. Use Proper Lighting: Natural light is ideal for photography, so try to take your photos during the day near a window. Avoid harsh overhead lighting or direct sunlight, as it can create shadows or glare. Consider using a lightbox or softbox to diffuse light evenly if natural light isn't available.

c. Choose the Right Background: Opt for a clean, neutral background that won't distract from the main focus of the image.

A plain white background is often preferred as it provides a professional look and allows the product to stand out.

d. Show Multiple Angles: Capture photos of the item from multiple angles to give buyers a comprehensive view. Include close-up shots of any important details or features to provide more context.

2. Enhancing Product Descriptions:

a. Be Descriptive: Write detailed and accurate product descriptions that provide essential information about the item. Describe its features, specifications, dimensions, materials, and any other relevant details.

b. Use Persuasive Language: Use persuasive language to highlight the benefits and unique selling points of the product. Focus on how it solves a problem or fulfills a need for the buyer.

c. Address Potential Concerns: Anticipate and address potential concerns or questions that buyers may have. For example, if selling clothing, provide sizing charts and measurements to help buyers choose the right size.

d. Include Keywords: Incorporate relevant keywords and phrases in your product descriptions to improve search visibility and attract potential buyers. Use terms that buyers are likely to search for when looking for products like yours.

3. Optimizing Image and Description Placement:

a. Prioritize Visuals: Place high-quality images prominently at the beginning of your listing to capture buyers' attention immediately. Use the gallery feature to showcase multiple images and give buyers a better understanding of the product.

b. Feature Key Information: Highlight important information in your product descriptions, such as product specifications, features, and benefits. Use bullet points or bold text to make key details stand out and easy to read.

c. Organize Information Effectively: Structure your product descriptions in a logical and easy-to-follow format. Break up long paragraphs into shorter, digestible sections to improve readability.

d. Include Calls to Action: Encourage buyers to take action by including clear calls to action in your listings. Use phrases like "Buy Now," "Add to Cart," or "Shop Now" to prompt immediate engagement.

4. Consistency and Branding:

a. Maintain Consistency: Keep your image style and description format consistent across all your listings to create a cohesive and professional brand image. Consistency helps build trust and familiarity with buyers.

b. Brand Your Listings: Incorporate your branding elements, such as logos, colors, and fonts, into your listings to reinforce your brand identity. Branding helps distinguish your listings from competitors and fosters brand recognition.

By following these strategies and techniques, you can effectively utilize high-quality images and descriptions to enhance your eBay listings, attract more buyers, and increase sales. Remember to regularly review and update your listings to reflect any changes or improvements to your products and maintain a competitive edge in the marketplace.

Chapter 4: Mastering Pricing and Profitability

Pricing Strategies: Finding the Sweet Spot

Setting the right price for your products is a critical aspect of successful selling on eBay. Finding the "sweet spot" – where your prices are competitive yet profitable – requires careful consideration of various factors. In this section, we'll explore effective pricing strategies to help you optimize your eBay listings and maximize your sales potential:

1. Research Market Trends:

a. Analyze Competitors: Start by researching your competitors' listings to understand their pricing strategies. Pay attention to similar products' prices, including their condition, features, and selling points.

b. Monitor Market Demand: Keep an eye on market trends and demand for your products. Use eBay's completed listings and sold items feature to analyze recent sales data and identify pricing trends.

2. Consider Your Costs:

a. Calculate Costs: Determine your total costs, including sourcing, shipping, eBay fees, and any other expenses associated with selling your products. Factor in your desired profit margin to ensure you're covering all costs and generating a profit.

b. Price for Profitability: Set your prices with profitability in mind. While competitive pricing is important, it's equally crucial to ensure your prices are sustainable and allow you to achieve your financial goals.

3. Utilize Pricing Strategies:

a. Competitive Pricing: Price your products competitively to attract buyers and stay competitive in the marketplace. Compare your prices to similar listings and adjust them accordingly to remain competitive.

b. Dynamic Pricing: Consider implementing dynamic pricing strategies, such as repricing tools or software, to adjust your prices in real-time based on market conditions, demand, and competition.

c. Bundle Pricing: Offer bundled or discounted pricing for purchasing multiple items together. Bundling products can increase the perceived value for buyers and incentivize larger purchases.

d. Loss Leader Pricing: Use loss leader pricing for certain products to attract buyers and drive traffic to your eBay store. Offer a discounted price on a popular item to encourage buyers to explore your other listings.

4. Test and Adjust:

a. A/B Testing: Experiment with different pricing strategies and variations to see which ones resonate best with your audience. Conduct A/B tests by listing the same product with different prices or pricing structures to gauge buyer response.

b. Monitor Performance: Regularly monitor your sales performance and analyze the impact of your pricing strategies. Pay attention to metrics such as conversion rates, average order value, and profit margins to assess the effectiveness of your pricing decisions.

5. Offer Additional Value:

a. Value-Added Services: Consider offering value-added services or incentives to justify higher prices for your products. This could include free shipping, extended warranties, or bonus items with purchase.

b. Build Trust: Establish trust and credibility with buyers by providing detailed product descriptions, high-quality images, and excellent customer service. Buyers are often willing to pay a premium for products from trusted sellers.

6. Stay Flexible and Adapt:

a. Stay Agile: Remain flexible and adaptable in your pricing strategies to respond to changes in market conditions, customer preferences, and competitive landscape.

b. Continuously Evaluate: Regularly evaluate and adjust your pricing strategies based on performance data, customer feedback, and market trends. Be open to refining your approach to maintain a competitive edge.

By implementing these pricing strategies and techniques, you can find the "sweet spot" for your eBay listings – where your prices are attractive to buyers while ensuring profitability for your business. Remember to regularly review and adjust your pricing strategies to stay competitive and maximize your sales potential in the ever-evolving marketplace.

Shipping and Handling: Providing Seamless Delivery

Efficient shipping and handling processes are crucial for ensuring customer satisfaction and driving repeat business on eBay. In this section, we'll delve into best practices and strategies to streamline your shipping and handling operations and provide a seamless delivery experience for your buyers:

1. Determine Shipping Methods:

a. Carrier Selection: Choose reliable shipping carriers that offer a balance between cost and service quality. Popular options include USPS, UPS, FedEx, and DHL. Compare shipping rates, delivery times, and additional services (e.g., tracking, insurance) offered by each carrier.

b. Shipping Services: Select appropriate shipping services based on the weight, size, and destination of your packages. Common options include standard shipping, expedited shipping, and priority mail. Consider offering free shipping or flat-rate shipping to attract buyers and simplify checkout.

2. Calculate Shipping Costs:

a. Shipping Calculators: Use eBay's shipping calculator or carrier-provided calculators to estimate shipping costs accurately. Factor in package dimensions, weight, destination, and selected shipping service to calculate shipping fees.

b. Handling Fees: Consider incorporating handling fees into your shipping costs to cover packaging materials, labor, and overhead expenses. Be transparent about handling fees in your listings to set clear expectations for buyers.

3. Package Items Securely:

a. Quality Packaging Materials: Use sturdy, protective packaging materials to safeguard your items during transit. Invest in appropriate boxes, bubble wrap, packing peanuts, and tape to prevent damage or breakage.

b. Secure Packaging: Pack items securely to minimize movement and reduce the risk of damage. Use padding and cushioning materials to fill empty spaces and provide cushioning against impact.

4. Provide Tracking Information:

a. Tracking Numbers: Always provide tracking numbers for shipments to enable buyers to monitor the delivery status of their orders. Upload tracking information promptly after shipping to keep buyers informed and build trust.

b. Automatic Tracking Upload: Take advantage of eBay's automatic tracking upload feature to streamline the tracking process. Link your eBay account with your shipping carrier to automatically upload tracking information for shipped orders.

5. Offer International Shipping:

a. Expand Your Reach: Consider offering international shipping to reach a broader audience of buyers worldwide. Evaluate the feasibility and cost-effectiveness of international shipping options based on your products and target markets.

b. Customs Declarations: Familiarize yourself with customs regulations and requirements for international shipments. Accurately complete customs declarations and provide detailed item descriptions to facilitate smooth customs clearance.

6. Optimize Handling Time:

a. Efficient Handling Processes: Streamline your handling processes to minimize handling time and ensure prompt order fulfillment. Organize your inventory, pack items efficiently, and schedule regular pickup or drop-off times with your shipping carrier.

b. Set Realistic Handling Times: Set realistic handling times in your listings based on your processing capabilities and shipping commitments. Consider factors such as order volume, holidays, and weekends when estimating handling times.

By implementing these shipping and handling best practices, you can provide a seamless delivery experience for your eBay buyers, enhance customer satisfaction, and build a reputation for reliability and professionalism. Continuously evaluate and optimize your shipping processes to adapt to changing market dynamics and meet evolving customer expectations.

Maximizing Profit Margins Without Sacrificing Sales

Achieving a balance between maximizing profit margins and maintaining sales volume is essential for sustainable growth and profitability on eBay. In this section, we'll explore strategies and tactics to optimize your pricing, operations, and sales processes to increase profitability without sacrificing sales:

1. Evaluate Pricing Strategies:

a. Competitive Analysis: Conduct a thorough analysis of competitors' pricing strategies to identify opportunities to adjust your prices while remaining competitive.

b. Dynamic Pricing: Implement dynamic pricing strategies using repricing tools or software to adjust prices in real-time based on market demand, competitor pricing, and other factors.

c. Price Bundling: Bundle complementary products together and offer them at a slightly discounted price compared to purchasing each item separately. This encourages larger purchases while maintaining overall profitability.

2. Optimize Operational Efficiency:

a. Inventory Management: Implement efficient inventory management practices to minimize carrying costs and reduce the risk of overstocking or stockouts. Use inventory management software to track inventory levels and forecast demand accurately.

b. Streamline Fulfillment: Streamline order fulfillment processes to reduce labor costs and shipping expenses. Optimize picking, packing, and shipping workflows to improve efficiency and reduce handling times.

c. Supplier Negotiation: Negotiate favorable terms with suppliers to secure better pricing, discounts, or favorable payment terms. Establish long-term relationships with reliable suppliers to leverage volume discounts and incentives.

3. Reduce Overhead Expenses:

a. Operational Expenses: Identify and eliminate unnecessary overhead expenses that do not directly contribute to sales or profitability. Review expenses such as office rent, utilities, and subscriptions to identify potential cost-saving opportunities.

b. Shipping Costs: Negotiate discounted shipping rates with carriers based on your shipping volume and frequency. Take advantage of bulk shipping discounts and shipping promotions offered by carriers to reduce shipping costs.

c. Marketing Spend: Evaluate the effectiveness of your marketing campaigns and allocate resources to channels that generate the highest return on investment (ROI). Focus on cost-effective marketing tactics such as email marketing, social media advertising, and content marketing.

4. Implement Upselling and Cross-Selling Strategies:

a. Upselling: Encourage customers to upgrade to higher-priced products or add premium features to their purchases. Highlight the benefits of upsell options and offer incentives such as discounts or promotions to incentivize upsells.

b. Cross-Selling: Recommend complementary or related products to customers based on their purchase history or browsing behavior. Showcase cross-sell items prominently on product pages and offer bundled discounts for purchasing multiple items together.

5. Focus on Customer Retention:

a. Exceptional Customer Service: Provide excellent customer service to build trust and loyalty with buyers. Address customer inquiries promptly, resolve issues effectively, and go above and beyond to exceed customer expectations.

b. Loyalty Programs: Implement customer loyalty programs or rewards programs to incentivize repeat purchases and foster long-term relationships with customers. Offer discounts, exclusive offers, or loyalty points for future purchases.

6. Monitor Key Performance Indicators (KPIs):

a. Profit Margin: Track your profit margins regularly to assess the impact of pricing adjustments and operational changes on profitability. Monitor both gross profit margins and net profit margins to understand your business's overall financial health.

b. Sales Volume: Monitor sales volume and trends to ensure that profitability improvements are not achieved at the expense of sales volume. Strike a balance between maximizing profit margins and maintaining sales growth.

By implementing these strategies and methods, you can effectively maximize profit margins without sacrificing sales on eBay. Continuously monitor and evaluate your pricing, operations, and sales processes to identify opportunities for improvement and optimize profitability over time.

Chapter 5: Maximizing Sales with eBay's Promotional Tools

1. Leveraging eBay's Promotional Tools:

eBay offers a range of powerful promotional tools to help sellers increase visibility, attract more buyers, and drive sales. Here's how to leverage these tools effectively:

- ➢ Promoted Listings: Utilize eBay's Promoted Listings feature to boost the visibility of your listings in search results and attract more potential buyers. With Promoted Listings, you can pay a small fee to have your listings displayed prominently in relevant search results and category pages. Set your advertising budget, choose the listings you want to promote, and eBay will display them to interested buyers, increasing your chances of making a sale. Monitor the performance of your promoted listings and adjust your advertising strategy based on data insights to maximize ROI.

- ➢ Markdown Manager: Take advantage of eBay's Markdown Manager tool to create limited-time sales and discounts on your listings. Markdown Manager allows you to easily schedule and automate price reductions, flash sales, and clearance events to incentivize purchases and create a sense of urgency among buyers. Choose specific items or entire categories to discount, set your sale prices, and promote your sales events to attract bargain-hunting buyers. Use compelling messaging and visuals to highlight your discounted prices and drive traffic to your listings during the sale period.

- ➢ Best Offer: Enable eBay's Best Offer feature to give buyers the flexibility to negotiate prices and make offers on your listings. Best Offer allows buyers to submit their best price for an item, giving you the opportunity to accept, decline, or counter their offers. Engage with potential buyers and negotiate mutually beneficial deals to increase sales and convert hesitant shoppers into satisfied customers. Use Best Offer strategically to encourage buyer engagement and drive sales while maintaining control over pricing and profitability.

- ➢ Volume Pricing Discounts: Implement volume pricing discounts to incentivize buyers to purchase multiple quantities of your items. eBay's Volume Pricing Discounts feature allows you to offer tiered discounts based on the quantity purchased, encouraging buyers to buy more and save. Set minimum quantity thresholds and discount levels for each tier, and eBay will automatically apply the discounts to eligible purchases. Volume pricing discounts can help increase average order value, reduce inventory turnover, and boost sales volume, ultimately driving higher revenue and profitability.

- ➢ Promotional Emails: Leverage eBay's Promotional Emails feature to reach out to potential buyers and drive traffic to your listings. Promotional Emails allow you to send targeted marketing messages and promotions to eBay users who have expressed interest in similar items or have previously interacted with your listings. Create compelling email campaigns with personalized messaging, exclusive offers, and calls to action to encourage recipients to visit your eBay store and make a purchase. Monitor the performance of your email campaigns and refine your targeting and messaging based on engagement metrics to optimize results.

By leveraging eBay's promotional tools effectively, you can increase visibility, attract more buyers, and drive sales for your eBay business. Experiment with different promotional strategies, monitor performance metrics, and refine your approach over time to maximize your sales potential and achieve your business goals.

2. Building Your Own Marketing Channels:

In addition to leveraging eBay's built-in promotional tools, sellers can create and manage their own marketing channels to further increase visibility, attract new customers, and drive sales. Here's how to build your own marketing channels effectively:

- ➢ Social Media Platforms: Establish a presence on popular social media platforms such as Facebook, Instagram, Twitter, and Pinterest to promote your eBay listings and engage with potential buyers. Create business profiles/pages for your eBay store and regularly share compelling content, including product highlights, promotions, behind-the-scenes glimpses, customer testimonials, and industry news. Use hashtags, tags, and relevant keywords to expand your reach and attract followers interested in your products. Encourage interaction, respond to comments and messages promptly, and build relationships with your audience to drive traffic to your eBay listings and convert followers into customers.

- ➢ Email Marketing: Build an email list of customers and prospects who have opted in to receive marketing communications from your eBay store. Use email marketing platforms such as Mailchimp, Constant Contact, or Klaviyo to create and send targeted email campaigns to your subscriber base. Segment your email list based on buyer preferences, purchase history, and demographics to deliver personalized content and offers. Send regular newsletters, promotional emails, product updates, and exclusive discounts to keep subscribers engaged and encourage repeat purchases. Track email performance metrics such as open rates, click-through rates, and conversion rates to measure the effectiveness of your campaigns and optimize future communications.

- ➢ Content Marketing: Develop a content marketing strategy to attract, educate, and engage your target audience through valuable, relevant, and informative content. Create blog posts, articles, guides, tutorials, videos, infographics, and other content formats related to your products, industry, or niche. Publish content on your own website or blog, guest post on relevant blogs or publications, and share content on social media platforms and email newsletters. Use content marketing to showcase your expertise, build credibility, and establish your eBay store as a trusted resource within your niche. Incorporate links to your eBay listings and store throughout your content to drive traffic and encourage conversions.

- ➢ Search Engine Optimization (SEO): Optimize your eBay listings, website, and content for search engines to improve visibility and attract organic traffic. Conduct keyword research to identify relevant search terms and phrases related to your products and target audience. Incorporate keywords strategically into your product titles, descriptions, and tags to enhance search engine rankings and increase exposure. Optimize your eBay store settings, including store categories, policies, and shipping details, to improve discoverability and relevance in search results. Monitor your search engine rankings, analyze traffic sources, and make adjustments to your SEO strategy to capitalize on emerging trends and opportunities.

By building your own marketing channels and diversifying your promotional efforts beyond eBay's platform, you can expand your reach, connect with new audiences, and drive sales growth for your eBay business. Experiment with different marketing channels, track performance metrics, and refine your strategies based on data insights and customer feedback to maximize your marketing effectiveness and achieve your business objectives.

2. Building Your Own Marketing Channels:

In addition to leveraging eBay's built-in promotional tools, sellers can create and manage their own marketing channels to further increase visibility, attract new customers, and drive sales. Here's how to build your own marketing channels effectively:

➤ Social Media Platforms: Establish a presence on popular social media platforms such as Facebook, Instagram, Twitter, and Pinterest to promote your eBay listings and engage with potential buyers. Create business profiles/pages for your eBay store and regularly share compelling content, including product highlights, promotions, behind-the-scenes glimpses, customer testimonials, and industry news. Use hashtags, tags, and relevant keywords to expand your reach and attract followers interested in your products. Encourage interaction, respond to comments and messages promptly, and build relationships with your audience to drive traffic to your eBay listings and convert followers into customers.

➤ Email Marketing: Build an email list of customers and prospects who have opted in to receive marketing communications from your eBay store. Use email marketing platforms such as Mailchimp, Constant Contact, or Klaviyo to create and send targeted email campaigns to your subscriber base. Segment your email list based on buyer preferences, purchase history, and demographics to deliver personalized content and offers. Send regular newsletters, promotional emails, product updates, and exclusive discounts to keep subscribers engaged and encourage repeat purchases. Track email performance metrics such as open rates, click-through rates, and conversion rates to measure the effectiveness of your campaigns and optimize future communications.

➤ Content Marketing: Develop a content marketing strategy to attract, educate, and engage your target audience through valuable, relevant, and informative content. Create blog posts, articles, guides, tutorials, videos, infographics, and other content formats related to your products, industry, or niche. Publish content on your own website or blog, guest post on relevant blogs or publications, and share content on social media platforms and email newsletters. Use content marketing to showcase your expertise, build credibility, and establish your eBay store as a trusted resource within your niche. Incorporate links to your eBay listings and store throughout your content to drive traffic and encourage conversions.

- Search Engine Optimization (SEO):Optimize your eBay listings, website, and content for search engines to improve visibility and attract organic traffic. Conduct keyword research to identify relevant search terms and phrases related to your products and target audience. Incorporate keywords strategically into your product titles, descriptions, and tags to enhance search engine rankings and increase exposure. Optimize your eBay store settings, including store categories, policies, and shipping details, to improve discoverability and relevance in search results. Monitor your search engine rankings, analyze traffic sources, and make adjustments to your SEO strategy to capitalize on emerging trends and opportunities.

By building your own marketing channels and diversifying your promotional efforts beyond eBay's platform, you can expand your reach, connect with new audiences, and drive sales growth for your eBay business. Experiment with different marketing channels, track performance metrics, and refine your strategies based on data insights and customer feedback to maximize your marketing effectiveness and achieve your business objectives.

3. Harnessing the Power of Social Media for eBay Success:

Social media platforms offer invaluable opportunities for eBay sellers to connect with their target audience, build brand awareness, and drive traffic to their listings. Here's how to harness the power of social media effectively for eBay success:

- ➤ Choose the Right Platforms: Identify the social media platforms that are most relevant to your target audience and industry. Popular platforms include Facebook, Instagram, Twitter, Pinterest, LinkedIn, and TikTok. Consider the demographics, interests, and behaviors of your ideal customers when selecting platforms to focus your efforts on.

- ➤ Create Compelling Profiles: Optimize your social media profiles to showcase your eBay store and offerings effectively. Use high-quality images, engaging descriptions, and relevant keywords to make a strong first impression. Include links to your eBay store, product listings, and website in your profile bios to drive traffic and facilitate conversions.

- ➤ Share Engaging Content: Create and share engaging content that resonates with your target audience and encourages interaction. Mix up your content with a variety of formats, including product photos, videos, infographics, blog posts, customer testimonials, and behind-the-scenes glimpses. Tailor your content to each platform's unique features and audience preferences to maximize engagement and reach.

- ➢ Promote Your eBay Listings: Showcase your eBay listings prominently on your social media profiles and posts to drive traffic and sales. Share product highlights, promotions, new arrivals, and exclusive offers with your followers to generate excitement and interest. Use compelling visuals, persuasive messaging, and clear calls to action to encourage clicks and conversions.

- ➢ Engage with Your Audience: Foster meaningful interactions with your audience by responding to comments, messages, and mentions promptly. Encourage conversations, ask questions, and solicit feedback to foster engagement and build relationships with your followers. Show appreciation for your followers' support and loyalty by acknowledging their contributions and offering personalized responses.

- ➢ Run Social Media Ads: Consider investing in paid advertising on social media platforms to expand your reach and target specific audience segments. Create targeted ad campaigns based on demographics, interests, behaviors, and retargeting to reach potential buyers who are most likely to be interested in your products. Monitor ad performance metrics, such as reach, engagement, click-through rate, and conversion rate, to optimize your campaigns and maximize ROI.

- ➢ Collaborate with Influencers: Partner with influencers, bloggers, or content creators in your niche to amplify your reach and credibility on social media. Identify influencers whose audience aligns with your target market and collaborate on sponsored content, product reviews, giveaways, or co-branded campaigns. Leverage influencers' expertise, authenticity, and influence to endorse your products and drive traffic to your eBay store.

By harnessing the power of social media effectively, eBay sellers can expand their reach, engage with their audience, and drive sales growth for their businesses. Experiment with different social media strategies, track performance metrics, and refine your approach based on insights and feedback to achieve your eBay success.

Chapter 6: Fostering Success Through Customer Satisfaction

1. The Importance of Customer Satisfaction:

Customer satisfaction is the cornerstone of a successful eBay business, playing a pivotal role in building trust, fostering loyalty, and driving repeat business. Here's why prioritizing customer satisfaction is crucial for your eBay success and how to achieve it:

- ➢ Builds Trust and Credibility: Satisfied customers are more likely to trust your eBay store and feel confident in their purchases. By consistently delivering high-quality products, excellent service, and positive shopping experiences, you can establish your reputation as a trustworthy seller within the eBay community.

- ➢ Encourages Repeat Business: Happy customers are more likely to return to your eBay store for future purchases and recommend your products to others. By exceeding customer expectations and consistently delivering exceptional value, you can cultivate a loyal customer base that drives sustained sales growth and revenue.

- ➢ Reduces Returns and Disputes: Providing excellent customer service and addressing buyer concerns promptly can help minimize returns, disputes, and negative feedback on your eBay account. By proactively addressing issues and resolving conflicts with professionalism and empathy, you can mitigate the risk of disputes and maintain a positive seller reputation.

- Enhances Brand Reputation: Positive customer experiences contribute to a favorable brand reputation and positive word-of-mouth marketing. By delivering on your promises, delighting customers with exceptional service, and fostering positive interactions, you can enhance your brand image and differentiate yourself from competitors in the marketplace.

- Drives Positive Feedback and Reviews: Satisfied customers are more likely to leave positive feedback and reviews for your eBay store, which can boost your seller rating, visibility, and credibility. Encourage satisfied customers to share their experiences and leave feedback by providing excellent service, requesting feedback politely, and expressing appreciation for their support.

Achieving Customer Satisfaction:

- Offer High-Quality Products: Ensure that the products you sell on eBay meet or exceed customer expectations in terms of quality, authenticity, and condition. Source products from reputable suppliers, conduct quality control checks, and accurately represent your items in listings to avoid buyer disappointment.

> Provide Excellent Customer Service: Prioritize responsive and helpful customer service to address buyer inquiries, resolve issues, and provide assistance throughout the purchasing process. Respond to messages promptly, offer clear and concise communication, and go above and beyond to exceed customer expectations.

> Honor Your Commitments: Fulfill your commitments to buyers by accurately describing products, shipping items promptly, and delivering orders on time. Be transparent about shipping times, return policies, and any potential issues that may arise to manage buyer expectations effectively.

> Solicit Feedback and Act on It: Actively seek feedback from buyers to understand their needs, preferences, and pain points. Use feedback surveys, reviews, and ratings to gather insights into customer satisfaction levels and identify areas for improvement. Incorporate feedback into your business practices to continuously enhance the customer experience.

> Personalize the Shopping Experience: Tailor your interactions with customers to their individual preferences and needs. Use personalization techniques such as addressing customers by name, recommending relevant products based on their purchase history, and sending personalized follow-up emails to foster a sense of connection and appreciation.

By prioritizing customer satisfaction and implementing strategies to exceed buyer expectations, you can cultivate a loyal customer base, drive positive word-of-mouth marketing, and achieve long-term success on eBay. Remember that satisfied customers are not only valuable assets but also ambassadors for your brand, contributing to your ongoing growth and success in the competitive e-commerce landscape.

2. Handling Inquiries and Resolving Issues:

Addressing buyer inquiries and resolving issues promptly and effectively is essential for maintaining high levels of customer satisfaction on eBay. Here's how to handle inquiries and resolve issues with professionalism and efficiency:

- ➢ Respond Promptly: Prioritize timely responses to buyer inquiries and messages to demonstrate your commitment to excellent customer service. Aim to respond to inquiries within 24 hours, if not sooner, to address buyer questions, concerns, and requests in a timely manner.

- ➢ Be Proactive: Anticipate potential issues or concerns that buyers may encounter during the purchasing process and proactively provide relevant information and assistance. Offer detailed product descriptions, sizing charts, shipping information, and return policies to address common questions and alleviate buyer uncertainty.

- ➢ Listen Actively: Take the time to listen actively to buyer feedback, concerns, and complaints to understand their perspectives and address their needs effectively. Empathize with buyers' frustrations or challenges and assure them that you are committed to finding a satisfactory resolution to their issues.

➢ Offer Solutions: Provide practical and actionable solutions to resolve buyer issues and concerns promptly. Offer options such as refunds, replacements, exchanges, or discounts to address defective or unsatisfactory products, shipping delays, or other issues that may arise during the transaction.

➢ Maintain Professionalism: Maintain a professional and courteous demeanor in all your interactions with buyers, even in challenging or confrontational situations. Stay calm, composed, and respectful, and refrain from engaging in heated arguments or confrontations that may escalate tensions and damage your reputation.

➢ Follow Up: Follow up with buyers after resolving their issues to ensure their satisfaction and address any lingering concerns or questions they may have. Express gratitude for their patience and understanding, and reassure them of your commitment to their satisfaction and continued support.

➢ Learn from Feedback: Use buyer feedback and inquiries as learning opportunities to identify areas for improvement and refine your business practices. Analyze common issues, patterns, and trends in buyer inquiries and feedback to address root causes and implement preventive measures to minimize future occurrences.

Document Communication: Keep detailed records of all buyer inquiries, messages, and interactions to track the resolution of issues and maintain transparency and accountability. Document agreements, commitments, and resolutions in writing to avoid misunderstandings and disputes later on.

By handling inquiries and resolving issues with professionalism, empathy, and efficiency, you can enhance customer satisfaction, build trust and credibility, and foster long-term relationships with buyers on eBay. Remember that effective communication, proactive problem-solving, and a commitment to customer-centricity are key pillars of a successful eBay business that prioritizes customer satisfaction above all else.

Turning Negative Feedback into Opportunities:

Negative feedback can be disheartening, but it also presents an opportunity to learn, improve, and demonstrate your dedication to customer satisfaction. Here's how to turn negative feedback into opportunities for growth and positive outcomes:

- Address Issues Promptly: When you receive negative feedback, acknowledge it promptly and publicly respond to the buyer's concerns with empathy and professionalism. Apologize for any inconvenience or dissatisfaction experienced by the buyer and assure them that you are committed to resolving the issue to their satisfaction.

- Offer Solutions Publicly: Whenever possible, offer solutions or remedies to address the buyer's concerns directly within the feedback forum. By demonstrating your willingness to resolve issues openly and transparently, you show potential buyers that you take customer satisfaction seriously and are proactive in addressing any issues that may arise.

- ➤ Seek to Understand: Take the time to understand the root cause of the negative feedback and identify any underlying issues or areas for improvement within your business processes. Consider reaching out to the buyer privately to gather more information and gain insights into their experience, preferences, and expectations.

- ➤ Implement Changes: Use negative feedback as constructive criticism to identify opportunities for improvement and implement changes to prevent similar issues from recurring in the future. Whether it's updating product descriptions, refining shipping procedures, or enhancing customer service protocols, prioritize actions that address the root causes of negative feedback and enhance the overall customer experience.

- ➤ Follow Up and Resolve: After addressing the buyer's concerns, follow up with them to ensure that they are satisfied with the resolution and to thank them for their feedback. Request that they consider revising their feedback to reflect the positive outcome of their experience. By demonstrating your commitment to making things right, you may be able to turn a dissatisfied customer into a loyal advocate for your business.

➤ Use Feedback as a Learning Opportunity: View negative feedback as a valuable source of insights and feedback that can help you identify blind spots, refine your processes, and elevate the quality of your products and services. Regularly review and analyze feedback trends to identify patterns, address recurring issues, and continuously improve your eBay business.

➤ Maintain a Positive Attitude: While negative feedback can be discouraging, it's essential to maintain a positive attitude and use it as motivation to excel. Embrace feedback as an opportunity for growth and development, and view each interaction as a chance to demonstrate your commitment to customer satisfaction and continuous improvement.

By effectively managing negative feedback and using it as an opportunity to enhance the customer experience, you can strengthen your reputation, build trust with buyers, and differentiate yourself as a seller who prioritizes customer satisfaction above all else. Remember that how you respond to negative feedback can ultimately shape your reputation and influence future buyers' perceptions of your eBay store.

Chapter 7: Streamlining Operations Through Outsourcing and Delegating Tasks

1. Outsourcing and Delegating Tasks:

Outsourcing and delegating tasks can be instrumental in streamlining operations, freeing up your time, and allowing you to focus on core aspects of your eBay business. Here's how to effectively leverage outsourcing and delegation to optimize efficiency and productivity:

- ➢ Identify Tasks for Outsourcing: Begin by identifying tasks within your eBay business that can be outsourced or delegated to third-party service providers or team members. These may include repetitive administrative tasks, customer service inquiries, product photography, listing optimization, order fulfillment, or accounting and bookkeeping tasks.

- ➢ Assess Skills and Expertise: Evaluate your own skills and expertise, as well as those of your team members or potential outsourcing partners, to determine the most suitable candidates for handling specific tasks. Consider factors such as experience, qualifications, availability, and cost when selecting individuals or agencies to outsource tasks to.

- ➢ Set Clear Objectives and Expectations: Clearly define the objectives, expectations, and deliverables for each outsourced task or project to ensure alignment and clarity. Provide detailed instructions, guidelines, and deadlines to communicate your requirements effectively and minimize misunderstandings.

- Select Reliable Service Providers: Choose reputable and reliable service providers, freelancers, or agencies with proven track records of delivering high-quality work and meeting deadlines. Conduct thorough research, read reviews, and request references or portfolios to assess their capabilities and reliability before committing to outsourcing agreements.

- Establish Effective Communication Channels: Establish open and transparent communication channels with outsourced team members or service providers to facilitate collaboration and exchange of information. Use project management tools, email, messaging apps, or video conferencing platforms to stay in touch, provide feedback, and address any issues or concerns that may arise.

- Monitor Progress and Quality: Regularly monitor the progress and quality of outsourced tasks or projects to ensure they meet your standards and expectations. Set milestones, checkpoints, and performance metrics to track progress and evaluate the effectiveness of outsourcing arrangements. Provide feedback and guidance as needed to course-correct and maintain alignment with your objectives.

- Maintain Accountability and Oversight: While outsourcing tasks can help streamline operations, it's essential to maintain accountability and oversight to ensure that delegated tasks are completed satisfactorily and in a timely manner. Establish clear accountability structures, assign responsibilities, and monitor performance to uphold standards of quality and efficiency.

> Evaluate Return on Investment (ROI): Continuously evaluate the return on investment (ROI) of outsourcing arrangements to assess their effectiveness and cost-effectiveness. Analyze factors such as time savings, productivity gains, cost savings, and the impact on overall business performance to determine the success of outsourcing initiatives and identify areas for optimization.

By strategically outsourcing and delegating tasks, eBay sellers can optimize their operations, leverage specialized expertise, and focus their time and resources on activities that drive growth and profitability. With careful planning, effective communication, and diligent oversight, outsourcing can be a valuable tool for streamlining processes, scaling operations, and achieving business objectives on eBay.

2. Expanding Your Product Range:

Diversifying your product range can open up new opportunities for growth, attract a broader audience, and increase sales potential on eBay. Here's how to expand your product range strategically:

> Conduct Market Research: Start by conducting comprehensive market research to identify emerging trends, popular product categories, and untapped niches within your target market. Analyze competitor offerings,

customer preferences, and market demand to uncover opportunities for expanding your product range.

➤ Assess Customer Needs: Understand your customers' needs, preferences, and buying behavior to identify complementary or supplementary products that align with their interests and purchasing habits. Solicit feedback from existing customers, analyze sales data, and monitor customer inquiries and requests to inform your product expansion strategy.

➤ Explore New Product Categories: Consider diversifying your product range by adding new product categories or expanding into related or complementary product lines. Look for synergies between existing and potential products to create cohesive product assortments that appeal to your target audience and encourage cross-selling opportunities.

➤ Source Reliable Suppliers: Identify reliable suppliers, wholesalers, manufacturers, or distributors for sourcing new products to add to your inventory. Establish relationships with reputable suppliers who offer high-quality products, competitive pricing, and reliable fulfillment services to ensure a seamless supply chain and consistent product availability.

Test New Products: Before committing to large quantities or investments, test new products or product lines to gauge customer interest, demand, and profitability. Consider launching pilot programs, limited-time promotions, or pre-order campaigns to assess market response and validate the viability of new products before scaling up production or inventory.

> ➢ Optimize Product Listings: Create compelling and informative product listings that highlight the unique features, benefits, and value propositions of your expanded product range. Use high-quality images, detailed descriptions, and relevant keywords to optimize visibility and searchability and attract potential buyers to your listings.

> ➢ Monitor Performance and Feedback: Continuously monitor the performance of your expanded product range, track sales metrics, and solicit customer feedback to evaluate the success of your product expansion efforts. Analyze sales trends, customer reviews, and return rates to identify top-performing products, optimize pricing strategies, and refine your product assortment over time.

> ➢ Iterate and Adapt: Be prepared to iterate and adapt your product range based on market dynamics, customer feedback, and performance metrics. Stay agile and responsive to changing trends, consumer preferences, and competitive pressures to capitalize on new opportunities and stay ahead of the curve in a rapidly evolving e-commerce landscape.

By strategically expanding your product range, eBay sellers can diversify revenue streams, mitigate risks, and capitalize on new market opportunities for sustainable growth and success. With careful planning, market insight, and strategic execution, product expansion can drive increased visibility, customer engagement, and sales revenue on eBay.

3. Streamlining Operations for Efficiency:

Efficient operations are essential for maximizing productivity, reducing costs, and optimizing performance in your eBay business. Here's how to streamline operations effectively:

- ➢ Identify Workflow Bottlenecks: Conduct a thorough analysis of your business processes to identify inefficiencies, bottlenecks, and areas for improvement. Map out the flow of tasks, inputs, and outputs across different stages of your operations to pinpoint opportunities for streamlining and optimization.

- ➢ Automate Repetitive Tasks: Leverage automation tools, software, and technologies to streamline repetitive, time-consuming tasks and free up your time for higher-value activities. Automate processes such as order processing, inventory management, customer communication, and data entry to reduce manual effort and minimize errors.

Implement Standard Operating Procedures (SOPs): Develop standardized procedures and protocols for performing routine tasks and operations within your eBay business. Document workflows, instructions, and best practices in SOPs to ensure consistency, efficiency, and compliance with established guidelines.

- Optimize Inventory Management: Implement efficient inventory management practices to optimize stock levels, minimize excess inventory, and prevent stockouts. Use inventory management software to track inventory levels, forecast demand, and automate reorder processes to maintain optimal inventory levels and reduce carrying costs.

- Streamline Order Fulfillment: Streamline order fulfillment processes to expedite order processing, reduce handling times, and improve customer satisfaction. Optimize picking, packing, and shipping workflows to minimize errors, reduce shipping costs, and expedite order delivery to customers.

- Invest in Technology: Invest in technology solutions and infrastructure to support efficient operations and scalability in your eBay business. Explore e-commerce platforms, order management systems, and integration tools that streamline operations, improve visibility, and enhance decision-making capabilities.

- Outsource Non-Core Activities: Consider outsourcing non-core activities or functions that are outside your area of expertise or require specialized skills. Delegate tasks such as accounting, bookkeeping, graphic design, or digital marketing to external service providers or freelancers to focus your time and resources on core business activities.

- Monitor Performance Metrics: Regularly monitor key performance indicators (KPIs) and performance metrics to track the effectiveness of your operational improvements and identify areas for further optimization. Measure metrics such as order processing time, fulfillment accuracy, customer satisfaction, and operational costs to assess performance and drive continuous improvement.

- Continuous Improvement: Foster a culture of continuous improvement within your eBay business by soliciting feedback from stakeholders, encouraging innovation, and actively seeking opportunities for optimization. Regularly review and refine your processes, policies, and procedures to adapt to changing market conditions and business requirements.

By streamlining operations for efficiency, eBay sellers can enhance productivity, reduce costs, and position their businesses for long-term success and growth. With a strategic focus on automation, standardization, and continuous improvement, sellers can optimize their operations and maximize the value they deliver to customers and stakeholders.

Chapter 8: Maximizing Revenue Through Cross-Selling and Upselling

1. Cross-Selling and Upselling Techniques:

Cross-selling and upselling are powerful strategies for increasing average order value, maximizing revenue, and enhancing the customer shopping experience on eBay. Here's how to leverage cross-selling and upselling techniques effectively:

- ➤ Understand Customer Needs: Start by understanding your customers' needs, preferences, and buying behavior to identify opportunities for cross-selling and upselling. Analyze purchase patterns, browsing history, and complementary product associations to recommend relevant products that add value and address customer needs.

- ➤ Bundle Products: Create product bundles or kits that combine complementary items or related products into cohesive packages. Bundle products together based on common use cases, themes, or customer preferences to offer convenience, value, and savings to buyers. Highlight the benefits of purchasing bundled products, such as cost savings or enhanced functionality, to incentivize upsells.

➢ Recommend Related Products: Use data-driven recommendations and personalized product suggestions to encourage cross-selling and upselling opportunities. Leverage eBay's recommendation algorithms and product recommendation widgets to showcase related products, similar items, or frequently bought together items to buyers based on their browsing and purchase history.

➢ Offer Discounts and Promotions: Incentivize cross-selling and upselling with discounts, promotions, or incentives for purchasing multiple items or upgrading to premium product versions. Offer percentage discounts, buy-one-get-one (BOGO) offers, or free shipping incentives to encourage buyers to add additional items to their cart or upgrade their purchase.

➢ Highlight Cross-Selling Opportunities: Highlight cross-selling opportunities within product listings, checkout pages, and confirmation emails to prompt buyers to consider complementary or supplementary products. Use persuasive copywriting, visual cues, and call-to-action buttons to draw attention to cross-selling suggestions and guide buyers toward additional purchases.

- **Provide Product Recommendations:** Offer personalized product recommendations and expert advice to assist buyers in finding the right products to meet their needs. Use features such as product comparison tables, size charts, compatibility guides, and product bundles to facilitate decision-making and add value to the shopping experience.

> Upsell Premium Versions or Add-Ons: Encourage buyers to upgrade to premium versions or add-ons of products by highlighting their superior features, benefits, or performance advantages. Showcase premium product versions, extended warranties, or accessory bundles as upsell opportunities to enhance value and increase order value.

> Use Social Proof: Leverage social proof and customer reviews to validate cross-selling and upselling recommendations and build buyer confidence. Showcase testimonials, ratings, and user-generated content that highlight the benefits and satisfaction of purchasing complementary or upgraded products to reassure buyers and overcome objections.

By implementing cross-selling and upselling techniques effectively, eBay sellers can maximize revenue, increase customer satisfaction, and drive long-term profitability. With a strategic focus on understanding customer needs, offering relevant recommendations, and providing value-added incentives, sellers can capitalize on cross-selling and upselling opportunities to enhance the shopping experience and achieve business success on eBay.

2. Establishing Partnerships and Collaborations:

Establishing partnerships and collaborations can be a strategic approach to expand your product offerings, reach new audiences, and drive cross-selling and upselling opportunities on eBay. Here's how to leverage partnerships effectively:

- ➤ Identify Potential Partners: Identify potential partners, suppliers, manufacturers, or brands whose products complement or enhance your existing offerings. Look for partners with complementary expertise, market presence, or customer base that aligns with your target audience and business objectives.

- ➤ Build Relationships: Invest time and effort in building strong relationships with potential partners through networking, outreach, and relationship-building activities. Attend industry events, trade shows, or networking events to connect with potential partners, and explore opportunities for collaboration and mutual benefit.

- ➤ Define Partnership Objectives: Clearly define the objectives, goals, and expectations of the partnership to ensure alignment and mutual understanding. Establish shared goals, KPIs, and success metrics that both parties are committed to achieving, and formalize agreements and contracts to outline roles, responsibilities, and terms of collaboration.

- ➤ Explore Co-Marketing Opportunities: Collaborate with partners on co-marketing initiatives, joint promotions, or co-branded campaigns to leverage each other's audience, reach, and resources. Co-create marketing collateral, content, or campaigns that showcase the value of complementary products or bundled offerings and promote them across multiple channels to maximize visibility and impact.

➤ Offer Exclusive Bundles or Discounts: Create exclusive product bundles, limited-time promotions, or special offers that are available exclusively through partnership channels. Offer partners unique incentives, discounts, or access to premium products to incentivize collaboration and encourage cross-promotion and upselling to their audience.

➤ Cross-Promote Products: Cross-promote each other's products or services through co-marketing efforts, social media shoutouts, email newsletters, or affiliate marketing programs. Showcase partner products alongside your own offerings and vice versa to introduce complementary products to each other's audience and drive cross-selling opportunities.

➤ Share Customer Insights: Share customer insights, data, and feedback with partners to inform product development, marketing strategies, and sales tactics. Collaborate on market research, customer surveys, or focus groups to gain valuable insights into customer preferences, pain points, and purchasing behavior that can inform joint initiatives and product offerings.

➤ Measure and Evaluate Performance: Monitor the performance of partnership initiatives, track key metrics, and evaluate the effectiveness of collaborative efforts. Measure the impact on sales, customer acquisition, and brand awareness to assess the ROI of partnerships and identify areas for optimization and improvement.

By establishing strategic partnerships and collaborations, eBay sellers can expand their product range, reach new audiences, and unlock cross-selling and upselling opportunities that drive revenue growth and business success. With a collaborative mindset, shared objectives, and mutual trust, sellers can leverage partnerships as a valuable tool for expanding their business and maximizing their impact on eBay.

3. Diversifying Income Streams Beyond eBay:

Diversifying income streams beyond eBay can help mitigate risks, expand revenue opportunities, and build a more resilient e-commerce business. Here's how to diversify your income streams effectively:

- ➢ Explore Multi-Channel Selling: Expand your online presence by selling on multiple e-commerce platforms in addition to eBay. Consider platforms such as Amazon, Etsy, Shopify, or Walmart Marketplace to reach new audiences, diversify your customer base, and reduce dependence on any single sales channel.

- ➢ Create Your Own Website: Establish your own e-commerce website or online storefront to sell directly to customers and retain greater control over your brand, pricing, and customer relationships. Use e-commerce platforms such as Shopify, WooCommerce, or

BigCommerce to build and customize your website easily.

- Launch Subscription Services: Introduce subscription-based offerings, membership programs, or recurring revenue models to generate predictable and recurring income streams. Offer subscription boxes, monthly product bundles, or exclusive access to premium content or services to incentivize customer loyalty and drive recurring revenue.

- Monetize Digital Products: Create and sell digital products, such as e-books, online courses, digital downloads, or software tools, to diversify your product offerings and generate passive income streams. Leverage your expertise, knowledge, and skills to develop valuable digital assets that appeal to your target audience.

- Explore Affiliate Marketing: Partner with affiliate programs or networks to promote third-party products or services to your audience and earn commissions on referred sales. Identify relevant affiliate opportunities within your niche or industry and integrate affiliate links or banners into your content or marketing channels to monetize traffic and referrals.

- Offer Services or Consulting: Monetize your expertise, skills, or knowledge by offering services or consulting to clients or businesses within your niche. Provide coaching, training, or consulting services related to your area of expertise, such as e-commerce, digital marketing, or product development, to diversify your income streams and leverage your expertise.

- ➢ Invest in Passive Income Streams: Explore passive income opportunities, such as rental properties, dividend-paying stocks, or digital assets, to generate additional revenue streams outside of your eBay business. Diversify your investment portfolio and build passive income streams that provide long-term financial stability and security.

- ➢ Evaluate New Business Ventures: Assess opportunities for launching new business ventures, side hustles, or entrepreneurial projects that complement your eBay business and leverage your skills, resources, and expertise. Explore new markets, industries, or business models that align with your interests and goals for diversifying income streams.

By diversifying income streams beyond eBay, sellers can reduce reliance on any single revenue source, mitigate risks, and unlock new growth opportunities for their e-commerce business. With a strategic approach to multi-channel selling, digital product creation, and passive income generation, sellers can build a more resilient and sustainable business that thrives in today's competitive landscape.

Chapter 9: Achieving Long-Term Success Through Continuous Learning and Skill Development

1. Continuous Learning and Skill Development:

Continuous learning and skill development are essential for staying competitive, adapting to change, and achieving long-term success as an eBay seller. Here's how to prioritize learning and skill development in your e-commerce journey:

- ➤ Stay Updated on Industry Trends: Keep abreast of industry trends, best practices, and emerging technologies in e-commerce, digital marketing, and online retail. Follow industry blogs, subscribe to newsletters, and attend webinars, conferences, or workshops to stay informed and gain valuable insights into the latest developments shaping the e-commerce landscape.

- ➤ Invest in Education and Training: Invest in formal education, training programs, or online courses to enhance your knowledge, skills, and expertise in areas relevant to your eBay business. Enroll in courses on e-commerce strategies, digital marketing tactics, product sourcing, inventory management, or customer service to deepen your understanding and proficiency in key areas.

- Seek Mentorship and Guidance: Seek mentorship and guidance from experienced e-commerce professionals, industry experts, or successful entrepreneurs who can offer valuable advice, insights, and support. Connect with mentors through networking events, industry associations, or online communities to learn from their experiences and benefit from their guidance.

- Experiment and Iterate: Embrace a mindset of experimentation and iteration by testing new strategies, tactics, and approaches in your eBay business. Be open to trying new ideas, learning from failures, and iterating on your processes to optimize performance and achieve better results over time.

- Develop Transferable Skills: Develop transferable skills that are valuable across various aspects of e-commerce and entrepreneurship, such as communication, problem-solving, critical thinking, and adaptability. Cultivate soft skills that enhance your effectiveness as a business owner and enable you to navigate challenges and seize opportunities effectively.

- Stay Customer-Centric: Prioritize understanding your customers' needs, preferences, and behaviors through market research, customer feedback, and data analysis. Continuously strive to improve the customer experience, anticipate their needs, and deliver value-added solutions that exceed their expectations and foster long-term loyalty.

- Network and Collaborate: Build relationships with fellow eBay sellers, industry peers, and business professionals through networking events, online forums, or social media groups. Collaborate on joint ventures, partnerships, or knowledge-sharing initiatives to exchange ideas, insights, and resources that contribute to mutual growth and success.

- Set Learning Goals: Set specific learning goals and objectives to guide your continuous learning journey and track your progress over time. Define measurable outcomes, milestones, and timelines for acquiring new skills, mastering new technologies, or achieving personal and professional development milestones.

- Stay Curious and Inquisitive: Cultivate a curious and inquisitive mindset that drives you to seek out new opportunities, explore different perspectives, and challenge the status quo. Ask questions, seek answers, and embrace a lifelong learning mentality that fuels your growth and evolution as an eBay seller and entrepreneur.

By prioritizing continuous learning and skill development, eBay sellers can adapt to evolving market dynamics, seize new opportunities, and position themselves for long-term success and sustainability in the ever-changing e-commerce landscape. With a commitment to ongoing growth and improvement, sellers can stay ahead of the curve, innovate their businesses, and thrive in competitive markets.

Chapter 10: Building a Strong Brand Identity

In today's competitive e-commerce landscape, building a strong brand identity is crucial for standing out from the crowd, fostering customer loyalty, and driving long-term success. Here's how to establish and cultivate a compelling brand identity for your eBay business:

1. Define Your Brand Identity:

- Clarify Your Brand Values: Start by defining your brand values, mission, and vision to establish the foundation of your brand identity. Consider what sets your eBay business apart, the principles you stand for, and the unique value proposition you offer to customers.

- Identify Your Target Audience: Understand your target audience's demographics, psychographics, and preferences to tailor your brand identity to resonate with their needs and aspirations. Develop buyer personas to gain insights into your ideal customers' motivations, pain points, and purchasing behavior.

- Craft Your Brand Story: Tell your brand story authentically and compellingly to connect with customers on an emotional level and create a memorable impression. Communicate the origins of your eBay business, your passion for your products, and the journey that led you to where you are today.

➤ Define Brand Elements: Develop visual and verbal brand elements that reflect your brand identity and create a cohesive brand experience across all touchpoints. Design a distinctive logo, choose a consistent color palette and typography, and establish brand voice and messaging guidelines that convey your brand personality and values.

2. Consistently Communicate Your Brand Message:

➤ Integrate Branding Across Channels: Ensure consistency in branding across all customer touchpoints, including your eBay listings, website, social media profiles, packaging, and customer communications. Maintain a unified brand presence that reinforces your brand identity and fosters recognition and trust among customers.

➤ Emphasize Brand Values: Showcase your brand values and commitments in your marketing efforts and communications to demonstrate authenticity, transparency, and social responsibility. Align your brand messaging with causes or issues that resonate with your target audience to forge deeper connections and differentiate your brand in the marketplace.

➤ Deliver Exceptional Customer Experiences: Provide consistently exceptional customer experiences that reflect your brand promise and values at every stage of the buyer journey. Exceed customer expectations with personalized interactions, prompt responses to inquiries, and seamless transactions that leave a lasting positive impression.

3. Cultivate Brand Loyalty and Advocacy:

- ➤ Engage and Delight Customers: Cultivate brand loyalty and advocacy by engaging with customers proactively, soliciting feedback, and addressing their needs and concerns promptly and effectively. Reward loyal customers with exclusive offers, discounts, or rewards programs to incentivize repeat purchases and referrals.

- ➤ Encourage User-Generated Content: Encourage customers to share their experiences with your brand through reviews, testimonials, and user-generated content on social media and review platforms. Leverage social proof and word-of-mouth marketing to build credibility, trust, and social validation for your brand.

- ➤ Foster Community and Connection: Create opportunities for customers to connect with your brand and with each other through community-building initiatives, such as online forums, social media groups, or customer appreciation events. Foster a sense of belonging and camaraderie among your customer base to deepen brand loyalty and strengthen relationships over time.

By defining a strong brand identity, consistently communicating your brand message, and cultivating brand loyalty and advocacy, you can differentiate your eBay business, foster customer loyalty, and build a lasting competitive advantage in the marketplace. Invest in building a brand that resonates with your target audience and reflects your values, vision, and commitment to excellence to position your eBay business for long-term success and growth.

Chapter 11: Mastering Customer Service Excellence

Exceptional customer service is the cornerstone of success in e-commerce, fostering customer satisfaction, loyalty, and advocacy. Here's how to master customer service excellence and elevate the buyer experience in your eBay business:

1. Prioritize Customer Satisfaction:

- ➤ Set High Service Standards: Establish high service standards and a customer-centric mindset throughout your eBay business. Make customer satisfaction a top priority and strive to exceed expectations at every touchpoint of the buyer journey.

- ➤ Respond Promptly: Respond to customer inquiries, messages, and feedback promptly and professionally. Aim to address customer concerns and resolve issues within a timely manner to demonstrate responsiveness and commitment to customer satisfaction.

- ➤ Personalize Interactions: Personalize customer interactions by addressing customers by name, acknowledging their preferences, and tailoring your communication to their specific needs and preferences.

Make customers feel valued and appreciated by offering personalized recommendations and assistance.

2. Provide Clear and Transparent Communication:

- Communicate Clearly: Communicate with customers clearly and transparently, providing accurate information about products, pricing, shipping, and policies. Use clear and concise language in your product listings, descriptions, and communications to avoid misunderstandings or confusion.

- Be Transparent: Be transparent about your business practices, policies, and processes to build trust and credibility with customers. Clearly communicate return policies, shipping times, and any potential issues or delays to manage customer expectations effectively.

3. Go Above and Beyond to Delight Customers:

- Offer Exceptional Service: Strive to go above and beyond to delight customers and exceed their expectations. Surprise and delight customers with unexpected gestures, such as handwritten thank-you notes, freebies, or personalized discounts, to create memorable experiences that foster loyalty and advocacy.

- Anticipate Customer Needs: Anticipate customer needs and proactively address them before they arise. Offer helpful resources, guidance, and assistance to customers to facilitate their decision-making process and enhance their overall shopping experience.

4. Handle Complaints and Resolutions Effectively:

- Listen Actively: Listen actively to customer feedback, complaints, and concerns, demonstrating empathy and understanding. Take the time to acknowledge customers' frustrations and validate their experiences before proposing solutions.

- Resolve Issues Quickly: Resolve customer issues and complaints promptly and effectively, aiming to turn negative experiences into positive outcomes. Offer solutions, refunds, or replacements as appropriate, and follow up to ensure customer satisfaction and loyalty.

5. Continuously Improve and Adapt:

- Seek Feedback: Solicit feedback from customers regularly to gather insights into their experiences and identify areas for improvement. Use customer feedback to refine your products, services, and processes and enhance the overall customer experience.

- Stay Agile: Stay agile and adaptable in response to changing customer needs, market trends, and business conditions. Continuously evaluate and optimize your customer service strategies and practices to stay ahead of the curve and deliver exceptional value to customers.

By mastering customer service excellence, eBay sellers can build trust, loyalty, and advocacy among their customer base, driving repeat business and long-term success. Prioritize customer satisfaction, communicate transparently, and go above and beyond to delight customers at every opportunity to differentiate your eBay business and create lasting value for your customers.

Data and analytics play a pivotal role in informing strategic decision-making, optimizing operations, and driving growth in e-commerce. Here's how to harness the power of data and analytics to gain actionable insights and drive success in your eBay business:

1. Collect and Analyze Key Metrics:

- Track Performance Metrics: Identify key performance indicators (KPIs) relevant to your eBay business, such as sales revenue, conversion rates, average order value, and customer acquisition cost. Use eBay's seller tools and analytics dashboards to track and analyze these metrics regularly to monitor performance and identify trends.

- Analyze Sales Data: Dive deeper into sales data to understand buying patterns, seasonal trends, and product performance. Analyze sales by category, time period, and customer segment to identify top-selling products, high-demand categories, and opportunities for growth.

2. Optimize Product Listings and Marketing Efforts:

➢ Use SEO Techniques: Optimize your product listings for search engines by incorporating relevant keywords, optimizing titles and descriptions, and leveraging eBay's search algorithm. Monitor keyword performance and adjust your listings accordingly to improve visibility and attract more organic traffic.

➢ Experiment with Marketing Channels: Experiment with different marketing channels and strategies, such as sponsored listings, social media advertising, or email marketing, to drive targeted traffic to your eBay listings. Analyze the performance of each channel and allocate resources to the most effective ones to maximize ROI.

3. Understand Customer Behavior:

➢ Analyze Buyer Behavior: Gain insights into customer behavior by analyzing data on browsing patterns, cart abandonment rates, and purchase history. Use this information to understand customer preferences, identify opportunities for cross-selling and upselling, and personalize marketing campaigns to target specific customer segments.

➢ Collect Feedback: Collect feedback from customers through surveys, reviews, and ratings to understand their satisfaction levels and gather insights into areas for improvement. Use feedback to refine product offerings, enhance the shopping experience, and build stronger relationships with customers.

4. Forecast Demand and Inventory Management:

➤ Utilize Predictive Analytics: Utilize predictive analytics techniques to forecast demand, anticipate market trends, and optimize inventory management. Analyze historical sales data, seasonality patterns, and market trends to make informed decisions about inventory levels, stock replenishment, and product sourcing.

➤ Minimize Stockouts and Overstock: Avoid stockouts and overstock situations by maintaining optimal inventory levels based on demand forecasts and sales projections. Use inventory management software to track stock levels, monitor reorder points, and automate replenishment processes to ensure product availability and minimize carrying costs.

Conclusion:

In conclusion, mastering the art of selling on eBay requires a multifaceted approach that encompasses strategic planning, effective marketing, exceptional customer service, and data-driven decision-making. By following the strategies outlined in this book, eBay sellers can unlock the full potential of their businesses, drive growth, and achieve long-term success in the dynamic world of e-commerce. Remember to stay adaptable, continuously learn and innovate, and prioritize the needs and satisfaction of your customers to thrive in the competitive marketplace. With dedication, perseverance, and a commitment to excellence, you can turn your eBay business into a profitable venture and realize your dreams of entrepreneurial success.

www.ingramcontent.com/pod-product-compliance
Lightning Source LLC
Chambersburg PA
CBHW050235230526
45470CB00005B/1957